POPSHOW
for Solo or Band

MW00743455

CONTENTS

** Correlated to the Belwin 21st Century Band Method, Level 1 and 2

INSTRUMENTATION

B21M0000	Conductor	B21M0011	Trombone
B21M0001	Flute	B21M0012	Baritone B.C.
B21M0002	Oboe	B21M0013	Baritone T.C.
B21M0003	Bassoon	B21M0014	Tuba
B21M0004	B♭ Clarinet	B21M0015	Keyboard Percussion
B21M0005	B♭ Bass Clarinet	B21M0016	Percussion
B21M0006	E♭ Alto Saxophone	B21M0017	Electric Bass
B21M0007	B♭ Tenor Saxophone	B21M0018	Guitar
B21M0008	E♭ Baritone Saxophone	B21M0019	Combined Percussion
B21M0009	B♭ Trumpet	B21M0000P	Piano Accompaniment
B21M0010	Horn in F	B21M0000CD	Compact Disc

AUGIE'S GREAT MUNICIPAL BAND

By JOHN WILLIAMS

Solo Arrangement

Band Arrangement

(Can be played after Lesson 5, Level 1 of the 21st Century Band Method)

LINUS AND LUCY

By VINCE GUARALDI

Solo Arrangement

Band Arrangement

(Can be played after Lesson 7, Level 1 of the Belwin 21st Century Band Method)

B21M0017

EYE OF THE TIGER

Words and Music by
FRANKIE SULLIVAN III and JIM PETERIK

(Can be played after Lesson 10, Level 1 of the Belwin 21st Century Band Method)

ALL I WANT FOR CHRISTMAS IS
MY TWO FRONT TEETH

Words and Music by
DON GARDNER

(Can be played after Lesson 12, Level 1 of the Belwin 21st Century Band Method)

B21M0017

TEQUILA

By CHUCK RIO

Solo Arrangement

Band Arrangement

(Can be played after Lesson 15, Level 1 of the Belwin 21st Century Band method)

B21M0017

FUN, FUN, FUN

Words and Music by
BRIAN WILSON and MICHAEL LOVE

Solo Arrangement

Band Arrangement

(Can be played after Lesson 18, Level 1 of the Belwin 21st Century Band method)

B21M0017

THE ROSE

By AMANDA McBROOM

Solo Arrangement

Band Arrangement

(Can be played after Lesson 18, Level 1 of the Belwin 21st Century Band method)

I'M WALKIN'

Words and Music by
ANTOINE DOMINO and DAVE BARTHOLOMEW

(Can be played after Lesson 2, Level 2 of the 21st Century Band Method)

HELENA POLKA

Traditional

Solo Arrangement

(Can be played after Lesson 4, Level 2 of the Belwin 21st Century Band Method)

B21M0017

Band Arrangement

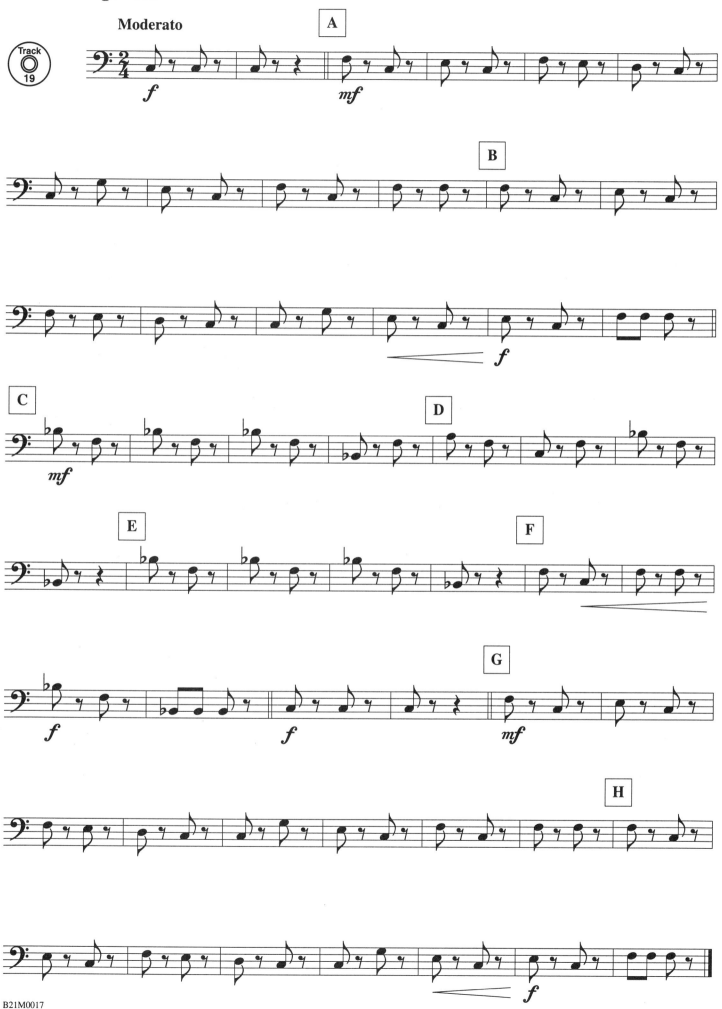

SING, SING, SING

Words and Music by
LOUIS PRIMA

Solo Arrangement

(Can be played after Lesson 13, Level 2 of the Belwin 21st Century Band Method)

B21M0017

Band Arrangement

STAR WARS (Main Theme)

Solo Arrangement

By JOHN WILLIAMS

Rhythm practice

(Can be played after Lesson 20, Level 2 of the Belwin 21st Century Band Method)

B21M0017

Band Arrangement

Theme From "SUPERMAN"

Solo Arrangement

By JOHN WILLIAMS

Band Arrangement

(Can be played after Lesson 20, Level 2 of the Belwin 21st Century Band Method)

B21M0017